P9-EDX-612

Bonnie
BLAIR

The Achievers

Bonnie BLAIR

GOLDEN STREAK

Cathy Breitenbucher

 Lerner Publications Company ▪ Minneapolis

*To Kent and Greta, who make me feel like a
champion every day.*

Information for this book was obtained from the author's interviews with
Bonnie Blair; Bonnie's mother, Eleanor; Bonnie's sister, Mary Blair Polaski;
Bonnie's brothers, Chuck and Rob Blair; Bonnie's teammate, Dan Jansen;
Bonnie's former coaches, Mike Crowe and Peter Mueller; Bonnie's coach,
Nick Thometz; and the following sources: *ABC Sports, Associated Press,
Barcelona/Albertville: The Official Publication of the U.S. Olympic Committee,
CBS Sports, Calgary Herald, Calgary Sun, Champaign, Ill., News-Gazette,
Chicago Tribune, The Complete Book of the Olympics, Los Angeles Times,
Milwaukee Journal, Milwaukee Sentinel, The 1984 Olympic Games:
Los Angeles/Sarajevo, The 1993 Sports Almanac, Olympian Magazine, Seoul/
Calgary 1988: The Official Publication of the U.S. Olympic Committee,
Sports Illustrated, Street & Smith's Olympic Magazine, United States International
Speedskating Association, United States Olympic Committee.*

This book is available in two editions:
Library binding by Lerner Publications Company
Soft cover by First Avenue Editions
241 First Avenue North, Minneapolis, Minnesota 55401

LIBRARY OF CONGRESS CATALOGING-IN-PUBLICATION DATA

Breitenbucher, Cathy.
    Bonnie Blair : golden streak / by Cathy Breitenbucher.
    p. cm. — (The Achievers)
    ISBN 0-8225-2883-5 : ISBN 0-8225-9665-2 (pbk.)
    1. Blair, Bonnie, 1964- —Juvenile literature. 2. Skaters—
United States—Biography—Juvenile literature. 3. Speed
skating—United States—Juvenile literature. [1. Blair, Bonnie,
1964- 2. Ice skaters. 3. Women—Biography. 4. Speed skating.]
I. Title. II. Series.
GV850.B63B74 1994
796.91'4'092—dc20   94-5744
[B]   CIP
                                                                AC
                                                               Rev.

Manufactured in the United States of America

1 2 3 4 5 6 - I/JR - 99 98 97 96 95 94

Contents

Making History

In the Winter Olympics, figure skating is the "flash" sport and speed skating is the "dash" sport. Figure skaters spend years perfecting their beautiful steps and spins. When it's time to compete, they put on dazzling costumes and pay close attention to their hairstyle and makeup. A figure skater not only has to perform well, he or she must look good, too.

Speed skaters, on the other hand, are judged only by the stopwatch. Their years of training are designed to produce the fastest, most efficient skating form. And they wear simple, lightweight, one-piece uniforms that are called "skins" because they are skintight. The uniforms fit tightly to the skater's body so that no air bubbles can get inside and slow down the speed skater.

Figure skaters and speed skaters don't even have their competitions on the same type of ice.

Figure skaters prefer ice that is slightly soft. That allows them to land their jumps gently. Speed skaters like the ice to be frozen just a few degrees colder so it is hard, fast, and slick.

No matter what the sport, athletes go to the Winter Olympics with high hopes. At the 1994 Olympic Games in Lillehammer, Norway, Bonnie Blair surpassed everyone's expectations.

In Bonnie's fourth trip to the Olympic Games, she earned two gold medals. Bonnie made Olympic history by winning the 500-meter and 1,000-meter races, giving her five gold medals in her career. That's more Olympic gold medals than any American woman in the entire history of the Winter *or* Summer Olympics. More than swimmer Janet Evans (4 golds) or track stars Florence Griffith Joyner (3), Jackie Joyner-Kersee (3), or even Evelyn Ashford (4)! "She is one of the greatest athletes in the history of our country," said Bonnie's happy coach.

Counting her one bronze medal, Bonnie has won more medals than any other U.S. athlete in Winter Olympics history. The previous record was five medals by Eric Heiden, another superstar speed skater. She is the only American woman to win gold medals in three consecutive Olympics.

"It's amazing to me," Bonnie said of her record-setting six-medal Olympic career.

In 1993, Bonnie was given the Sullivan Award as the best amateur athlete in any sport in the United States. Stacey Sullivan (left) presented the trophy to Bonnie and her mother, Eleanor (right).

Bonnie demands perfection from herself. Her best is usually unbeatable. In the six years leading up to the 1994 Games, the world record in the 500 meters belonged to Bonnie for all but two months. "I might not always be at the top," said Bonnie, "but during the Olympic years I have been skating very well."

Bonnie works out in a Milwaukee ice arena.

Bonnie skates faster than the very best male track stars can run. Her world record in the 500 meters is 38.99 seconds. Even if legendary Olympic sprinter Carl Lewis could string together five races equal to his 100-meter world record, his time still would be more than 10 seconds slower than Bonnie's.

Olympic speed skating races like Bonnie's take place on an oval-shaped ice rink. The oval is 400 meters around, the same size as a running track around a football field. It looks big, but the oval has only two lanes for racing. Skaters compete two at a time, in a pair. No matter which skaters are in the pair, everyone competes against the clock. Each skater gets only one try. The skater with the best time after all the pairs have raced wins.

Speed skaters are among the fastest athletes in any sport in the world. Year-round training builds their strong legs. They wear skates with blades that are 12 to 18 inches long and razor sharp. By pushing to the side with powerful strokes, speed skaters can zoom around a 400-meter oval track at about 35 miles an hour.

Speed skaters lean forward at the waist for their entire race. That way, the air will pass over their backs the same way air passes over the top of an airplane. The skaters keep their backs straight and their heads up, eyes looking forward. In the 500 meters, they swing their arms vigorously from side to side for the entire race to increase their speed. In longer races, the skaters sometimes put one arm flat against their back to conserve their energy. Speed skating is hard work, but Bonnie makes it look natural.

Speed skaters and coaches all around the world marvel at Bonnie's skating style. She reacts quickly to the starter's gun. She flies down the opening stretch faster than any woman in the world. She powers around the turns, always maintaining perfect form. And she puts all her effort into every stroke until she hits the finish line.

Away from the rink, Bonnie is funny and friendly. She loves to golf, bake cookies, and watch television. She is a generous person too. In 1993 she helped unload truckloads of bottled water for victims of flooding in the Midwest, and she raises money for many charities.

But when it's time to go to the starting line at a speed skating meet, a fire burns inside Bonnie. She focuses so intently on her race that she usually doesn't hear the screaming crowds. "She's got an incredible head for competition," says her friend and Olympic teammate Dan Jansen. "She always races well."

Especially at the Olympics!

Born to Skate

A lot of people get an early start on their athletic careers. But Bonnie Blair got an earlier start than most. In fact, she almost was born at an ice rink!

Bonnie's family was involved in speed skating long before she was born. Her parents, Eleanor and Charlie Blair, were ice skaters when they were growing up, and they taught their first five children to skate, too. A neighbor introduced two of the children to speed skating, and soon the whole Blair family was involved in the sport.

Around the Blair household in Cornwall, New York, winter Wednesday evenings were reserved for speed skating meets. There were divisions for beginners (known as Tiny Tots), for experienced skaters, and even for adults. All evening, skaters zoomed around the hockey rink.

Every Wednesday, the Blairs went to the races.

Eleanor and Charlie Blair taught their children to be responsible for getting their equipment and racing suits together for the one-hour drive to the rink. Eleanor Blair liked watching her children race. Like a lot of the skaters' dads, Charlie Blair volunteered as an official at the meets. He was also a big fan. No matter what his kids' skating results were, he was always there with a pat on the back. "Go get 'em next time," he'd say.

Skating was a way of life in the Blair family for many years. The oldest two children, Chuck and Mary, competed before they grew up and moved away. In 1964, Chuck was in the Air Force and Mary was away at college. "Team Blair" then consisted of 15-year-old Suzy, 8-year-old Rob, and 7-year-old Angela. Until March 18, that is.

That evening, the Blair children planned to race at a meet in Yonkers, New York. But Eleanor wasn't feeling well. She was expecting a baby, the family's sixth child, any day. She decided it might not be a good idea for her to go along to the competition after all.

The hospital was on the way to the ice rink. In those days, most fathers didn't go into the delivery room when their children were born. So Charlie dropped Eleanor off at the hospital, then went on with the three children to the skating meet.

Suzy, Rob, and Angela didn't worry about their

mother being alone at the hospital. They didn't understand that at Eleanor's age (45), having a baby could present special medical problems. All they understood was that they had races to skate and they didn't want to be late.

Soon, however, the Blairs forgot all about their skating plans. Barely an hour after Eleanor arrived at the hospital, a healthy baby was born. A call was made to the ice rink. Then, the public address announcer told everyone there that the Blair family had a new girl skater. People began congratulating Charlie and the Blair children.

For once, the Blairs didn't spend the entire evening at the speed skating meet. They quickly gathered up their equipment and drove back to the hospital. They were eager to see the little girl—baby Bonnie had arrived!

When Bonnie was just a few months old, Charlie Blair, who worked as a civil engineer, was transferred to Champaign, Illinois. Now the ice rink wasn't an hour away from the Blairs' home—it was just across town.

Champaign is well known as the home of the University of Illinois. The university's ice arena had been used by speed skating clubs for many years. Coaches from Champaign took their best skaters to meets against teams from all over the state.

The Blair family (clockwise from upper left): Eleanor, Mary holding Bonnie, Charlie, Angela, Rob, and Suzy.

When Bonnie was just two years old, Suzy, Rob, and Angela decided it was time for her to learn to skate. Many children start out on little skates that are strapped onto their shoes. These skates are called double-runners because they have two blades side by side, about an inch apart, that make it easier for the child to stand up.

The Blair kids, though, didn't want Bonnie to use double-runners. They found the smallest skates they had around the house, a pair they all had worn as youngsters, and slipped them on over Bonnie's shoes. The fit was perfect! With the help of her older brother and sisters, Bonnie stood on skates for the first time. Then she learned how to take a few steps. It wasn't long before Bonnie was skating for real.

Bonnie, almost three, gets skating help from her dad.

Dedicating Herself

Bonnie loved to skate, but there were other things to see and do at the rink, too. At first, the noisy Zamboni machine frightened her when it circled around the rink, making the ice shiny and slick. Her brother's and sisters' friends loved to buy her treats, so Bonnie sometimes spent more time at the snack bar than on the ice. And some meets lasted so long, Bonnie would get worn out and need a nap. In fact, a few times she curled up on her mom's lap and slept right through her Tiny Tots races.

By the time she was in grade school, though, skating was Number 1 with Bonnie. Whenever it was time to go to the rink, Bonnie would race out the door so she could be the first one in the car. Sure, she loved singing in school programs and going to slumber parties with her friends, but on the weekends she wanted to be on the ice.

Bonnie learned to sharpen her own skates when she was 11. Watching her are Rob, Charlie, and Eleanor.

Most of the time, Bonnie raced on a hockey rink. Races on hockey rinks are called short-track events because each lap is only about 100 meters. Short-track events also are called pack-style races because there are four or more skaters on the ice at once. The skaters must finish among the leaders in preliminary races, called heats, to qualify for the final race. In the final, the first skater to cross the finish line wins.

20

Sometimes Bonnie's races were held in Milwaukee, Wisconsin, about a 4½-hour drive from Champaign. Skaters from all over the Midwest wanted to race in Milwaukee because the rink there was a 400-meter oval—just like in the Olympics. Instead of racing in a pack, skaters in Milwaukee competed just two at a time. That is long-track skating. Officials keep track of everyone's times, and after all the skaters have raced, the officials compare their times and declare a winner.

Skating in Milwaukee was a lot harder than skating in Champaign. The Milwaukee rink was outdoors, and sometimes the wind blew so hard it seemed as if Bonnie would get lifted right off the ice and fly away like Mary Poppins! Still, Bonnie's dad believed in her. "You'll be in the Olympics someday," he told her.

When Bonnie reached high school age, she was the only one of the Blair children still living at home. It was strange not to have a whole house full of skaters. Bonnie was a cheerleader at Centennial High School and a member of the student council. She liked being involved in school activities, but she liked skating, too. She was having a tough time deciding how to spend her free time.

Then, a new "big sister" came along. She was Cathy Priestner, a Canadian speed skater who had won a silver medal in the 1976 Olympics.

Cathy moved to Champaign in 1979, when Bonnie was 15, and noticed her one day at the university ice arena. Cathy saw Bonnie's potential, and soon she was helping Bonnie train. Every day at 6 A.M., Cathy and Bonnie met at the rink for a practice. The manager gave them a key so they could get into the rink by themselves and skate before Bonnie went to school each morning.

The 1980 U.S. Olympic trials were only a few months away. Skaters earn places on the Olympic team by doing well at the trials. Cathy wanted Bonnie to skate fast enough to qualify for the trials. After all their early-morning sessions, Bonnie did!

The Olympic trials were the biggest event Bonnie had ever skated in. Only 15 years old, she was one of the youngest skaters there. She didn't qualify for the Olympics that time, but she learned something important. She now knew that if she applied herself, she could do better than she'd ever thought she could. It would mean sacrifices. She gave up her spot as a cheerleader so she could go to Milwaukee every weekend. She began lifting weights with the Centennial High football team and training year-round. Because she was a good student, she was allowed to graduate in the middle of her senior year and focus on her skating. Soon, everyone in Champaign knew Bonnie was serious about making the 1984 Olympic team.

Champaign policemen Sergeant Dan Strand (left) and Detective Jerry Schweighart (right) were some of Bonnie's first fans.

A group of police officers—Sergeant Danny Strand, Detective Jerry Schweighart, and Patrolman Jerry Ehrsham—heard about Bonnie, too. They wanted teenagers in Champaign to know that police officers are their friends, so they decided to help Bonnie. They told her they would help raise money so she could move to Milwaukee and practice with other good young skaters. During the first year, the officers raised $7,000 for "Champaign Policemen's Favorite Speeder."

23

Everyone's efforts paid off when Bonnie skated at the Olympic trials. This time, she earned a spot on the U.S. team for the 500-meter race. Bonnie would be competing in the 1984 Winter Olympics in Sarajevo, Yugoslavia.

Sarajevo has been nearly destroyed in a war that began after Yugoslavia split into several countries in 1991. In 1984, however, the people of Sarajevo hosted the Olympic Winter Games, which promote peace and friendship.

The U.S. team members went to Sarajevo knowing some people expected them to match the success of the 1980 Olympic squad. In Lake Placid, New York, four years earlier, Eric Heiden had won all five men's speed skating events, Leah Poulos Mueller had earned two silver medals, and Eric's sister, Beth, had taken a bronze. Plus, the American hockey team had won the hearts of the entire nation by unexpectedly winning the gold medal. Soon after the 1980 Olympics, Eric, Leah, and Beth retired from competition. The 1984 U.S. speed skating team was young and inexperienced.

Bonnie was realistic about her chances as she prepared for the Olympics. After all, she had been competing against the best skaters in the world for only a year. "I go into every race hoping it will be better than the last one," she said before the Games.

At every Winter Olympics, the organizers worry that not enough snow will fall for the skiing events. Sarajevo had the opposite problem. The morning of February 10, a foot of snow fell. Gusty winds forced organizers to postpone the men's downhill ski race scheduled for that day. But, after a 5½-hour delay, the snow was plowed off the Zetra Speed Skating Oval, and the women's 500-meter speed skating race went on.

With snow swirling around the oval, everyone thought record times would be all but impossible. Everyone, that is, except Christa Rothenburger. She defeated her East German teammate, defending champion Karin Enke, for the gold medal. Rothenburger skated an Olympic-record 41.02 seconds, and Enke was timed in 41.28. The bronze medalist, Natalya Chive of the Soviet Union, finished in 41.50.

Seventeen years after her brother and sisters slipped her feet into skates for the first time, Bonnie placed eighth in the Olympic Games. Her time was 42.53 seconds.

"People look only at the medals," Bonnie said later. "We were right there. The times are so close. One little slip can cost you a medal."

After the Olympics, Bonnie set out to narrow that gap. If she could fine-tune her form, she could be one of the very fastest skaters in the world.

One way for Bonnie to become tougher mentally was to go back to short-track, or pack-style, speed skating, like the races she had competed in as a child. In short-track, a skater has to be smart enough to avoid bumping into another skater and falling down.

Bonnie always had been very good at short-track skating. The sport was not yet part of the Olympics, but it was included in the National Sports Festival, a kind of Olympics for American athletes. (The National Sports Festival now is called the U.S. Olympic Festival.)

The 1985 National Sports Festival, in Baton Rouge, Louisiana, gave Bonnie a chance to shine in short-track skating. She won gold medals in all four women's races on the schedule. Then she did even more. When one of the skaters on a men's relay team was injured, Bonnie was invited to compete in a men's event. That was all the challenge she needed! Bonnie's team not only won the gold medal in the 5,000-meter relay, it shattered the Sports Festival record by more than 13 seconds.

The victory made Bonnie the top gold-medal winner in any sport that year at the Sports Festival. "I never thought I could win five golds," she said. "This is just terrific."

In 1986 she captured the world championship in short-track skating by winning three of the four

events. But to become an Olympic champion, Bonnie needed to train for the long-track races. The best places to practice were in Europe, because the outdoor skating ovals there opened earlier in the year than the oval in Milwaukee did. But going to Germany or Switzerland for a couple of months every year was expensive.

Fortunately, Bonnie's brother Rob stepped in to help. Rob was a college friend of professional basketball player Jack Sikma, who played for the Seattle SuperSonics and the Milwaukee Bucks. Rob, Jack, and some other friends agreed to start a fund to help pay Bonnie's bills. Combined with the money from the Champaign police officers, Bonnie's bank account now was big enough that she could travel to the best training sites.

Bonnie became a celebrity in the Netherlands and Norway, where speed skating is as popular as baseball, football, and basketball are in America. Whenever Bonnie skated in Heerenveen, Netherlands, the rink would be packed with 16,000 spectators, who would sing "My Bonnie Lies Over the Ocean" to her. As if to thank those fans, Bonnie set a world record in Heerenveen at the end of the 1987 skating season.

Bonnie had come a long way from the early-morning practice sessions in Champaign, Illinois. She was a veteran of hundreds of races, had won medals in world competitions, and was a world-record holder. She was counting down the days to the 1988 Winter Games.

Victory in Calgary

Even before the 1988 Winter Olympics in Calgary, Bonnie was becoming well known in the United States. Her picture was on the cover of *Life* magazine. Dozens of reporters from all over the world interviewed her for their newspapers. President Reagan heard about Bonnie, too, and wanted her to come to dinner at the White House just a few days before the Games started. But Bonnie turned down the invitation. She needed to concentrate on her training.

Calgary, which is in the province of Alberta in western Canada, was eager for the Olympics to begin, too. It was the first Canadian city to host the Winter Games. The years of planning showed when the Olympics opened on February 13.

Bonnie and other athletes marched into huge McMahon Stadium early in the opening ceremony and took their seats at one end of the stadium.

From there, they had a terrific view of the entertainment, which included Native Americans on horseback and square dancers in colorful costumes and earmuffs. The thrilling program was capped by the arrival of the Olympic flame. Bonnie was excited to see Cathy Priestner, who had inspired her to pursue Olympic-style skating, help carry the torch into the stadium.

After that, though, Bonnie saw few people around Calgary. Athletes were scurrying around the Olympic Village, her family was in town for the Games, and the entire city was buzzing with excitement. But Bonnie spent most of the first week of the Olympics in her room. Of course, she had to eat and go to practice every day, but most of the time Bonnie stretched out on her bed at the Olympic Village and watched the Olympics on television.

"I don't really think too much about the pressure," Bonnie said just before the Olympics. "I just worry about myself and what I have to do, day to day. I take each weekend or competition one at a time."

On the first day of Olympic competition, Bonnie's good friend and teammate, Dan Jansen, was told that his older sister was about to die of leukemia. Just a few hours later, Dan fell in his 500-meter race and did not finish.

Bonnie works out with her friend and teammate, Dan Jansen.

He also fell in his 1,000-meter race four days later. Dan, who was the reigning world champion, left the Olympics without any medals.

"That was the most difficult thing that happened to the whole team," Bonnie said. "He had the two worst races of his life." Eric Flaim won a silver medal in the 1,500 meters for the United States, but the American team was anxious for a gold.

Finally, Bonnie's big chance arrived. She was so excited she could hardly eat all day. The only thing that sounded good was a peanut butter-and-jelly sandwich, so she made one for herself at the Olympic Village and tried to relax.

Meanwhile, the stands around the Olympic Oval were filling up quickly for the women's 500-meter race. The trip to Sarajevo in 1984 had been so expensive that only Bonnie's mother and her sisters Mary and Suzy had been there. This time, though, the Olympics were like a Blair family reunion. Her dad and mom both came from Champaign, along with Bonnie's brother Chuck. Her brother Rob flew in from Texas. Her sisters made the trip, too—Suzy from Oregon; Angela from Connecticut; and Mary from Colorado. In all, there were 19 family members and friends of Bonnie's at the Olympics!

Bonnie's fan club arrived early to hang signs for her. One of them was from a tiny fan who was attending the Olympics. That sign read: "Dear Aunt Bonnie, Skate Fast. Love, Brittany." Brittany was Rob Blair's 4½-month-old daughter.

Other athletes were eager to see the races. Brian Boitano, who had won the men's figure skating title, came to watch. So did Katarina Witt, who later would win the gold in women's figure skating. Members of the U.S. speed skating team stood along the mats that circled the track.

Many of the other U.S. Olympic athletes cheered for Bonnie when she was competing, and she returned the favor by encouraging them during their races and events.

For the first time in Olympic competition, speed skating races were being held on an indoor rink. With no wind or snow to slow them down, the skaters in Calgary were rewriting the record books.

For Bonnie, the indoor ice was a blessing. Just 5 feet, 4½ inches tall, Bonnie skates her best when the air is still and the ice is clean. And in Calgary, the ice was so clean it shone like a pane of glass.

At the Olympics, speed skaters are divided into three groups based on their best times. Then a draw determines exactly when the skaters will race and assigns them to the inner or outer lane. Because the inside lane is slightly shorter than the outside lane, skaters change lanes each time they reach the crossing straight, which is the straight-away opposite the finish line. That way, both skaters skate the same distance. The skater who begins the 1¼-lap 500 meters on the inner lane finishes on the outer lane. Most skaters have trouble moving at top speed on the tight inner lane, so they prefer to finish in the outer lane.

When the pairings were drawn for the race, Bonnie was placed in the fourth one, starting in the inner lane. Her main rival, defending champion Christa Rothenburger of East Germany, was in the second pair, also starting in the inner lane. Karin Enke Kania, who had won the Olympic gold medal in 1980, was in the fifth pair and would start in the outer lane. Although there were 15 pairs of skaters who would race, the experts predicted that the three medalists would come from the first five pairs.

From left, Karin Kania, Bonnie, and Christa Rothenburger
were friendly rivals.

Rothenburger had every reason to be confident
as she glided to the starting line. She was the
defending Olympic champion and had broken Bonnie's world record in a pre-Olympic meet at the
Calgary rink. Now, when it counted the most,
Rothenburger roared off the starting line. She
passed the first 100 meters and the announcer
called out her time of 10.57 seconds. When the
race was over, Rothenburger had yet another
world record—39.12 seconds.

The tension built while the third pair raced. Then came Bonnie's turn. She took off her warm-up jacket and pants to reveal her silver-and-orange striped racing suit. An official helped her put on the white arm band signifying that she would begin the race in the inner lane. Bonnie and Zofia Tokarczyk of Poland were called to their starting positions.

Then—pow! The gun went off and the race was on. The noise in the Olympic Oval rose to a bone-jarring level as Bonnie's fans yelled and clapped and stomped their feet. Somehow, Bonnie heard the announcer call out her 100-meter time—10.55 seconds. That was two-hundredths of a second faster than Rothenburger's 100-meter time! The sound got even louder as Bonnie bore down on the backstretch, her hands slicing through the air. Then came that last 100-meter straightaway and the cheering was so loud it seemed as though the roof would come off the gigantic building.

As Bonnie crossed the finish line, everyone looked at the scoreboard. In an instant, it registered her time: a world-record 39.10 seconds. Bonnie was in first place! She thrust her fists into the air and coasted around the track. Her coach offered her a high five. Bonnie's boyfriend gave her a hug, and so did Cathy Priestner, who now worked at the Calgary Olympic Oval. "I think I just got it on guts," Bonnie said later.

Overcome by joy and relief, Bonnie sat and cried while the fifth pair skated. Kania posted an outstanding time of 39.24 seconds, but that was fast enough for only the bronze medal. After that, no other skater was even close to Bonnie's time. Bonnie Blair was the new Olympic champion!

Four days later, Bonnie competed again, in the 1,000 meters. This time, she was in the second pair of the night. Both Kania and Rothenburger would skate after her, so they would know exactly how fast they'd need to go to beat Bonnie.

Bonnie finished with an Olympic record of 1 minute, 18.31 seconds. Kania, however, came up with a world record of 1:17.70 to bump Bonnie into second place. Then Rothenburger blazed to yet another world record, 1:17.65. The same three skaters climbed the victory stand as in the 500 meters, but this time Rothenburger was on top, Kania was in the silver-medal position, and Bonnie stood on the third step.

Though she had two medals, Bonnie's Olympics weren't over yet. She had one more race—the 1,500 meters, her weakest event—the following night. Pair by pair, the Olympic record went lower and lower. Bonnie skated in the seventh pair, and with one lap to go she had the fastest time of the night. But she couldn't keep up her grueling pace, and her final time put her in a distant fourth place.

The next night, Bonnie carried the U.S. flag into McMahon Stadium for the closing ceremony. The captains for the U.S. teams all voted to give Bonnie the honor because she was the only American to win two medals.

Soon after the Olympics, Bonnie got another chance to visit the White House. In fact, the whole American team was invited. Bonnie presented a U.S. Olympic team jacket to President Reagan.

"I'm glad I'm able to represent the U.S.," she said at the Olympics. And with two trips to the medalists' podium, what a job she had done for her country.

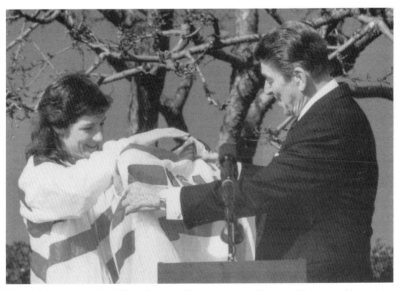

Bonnie presents President Reagan with an Olympic jacket.

Bonnie works out on in-line skates during her off season.

Twice a Winner

Even in non-Olympic years, speed skaters stay busy preparing for the world championships and other important meets. During the five-month season, speed skaters compete in about 25 races. In the four years between the Calgary and Albertville Olympics, Bonnie was busier than most of her American teammates.

After the Calgary Olympics, Bonnie attended Montana Tech in Butte, Montana, and trained on an oval there. She won the world sprint speed skating championship. She also tried bicycle racing one summer. She competed against the top riders from all over the United States and placed fourth or fifth in every race she entered. But Bonnie worried that she could get injured if she crashed during a bicycle race, so she gave up that sport.

Companies flew Bonnie around the country to talk to their employees about her winning spirit.

Bonnie and other speed skaters use the Brewers' parking lot for a workout.

She rode in the parade at the Indianapolis 500. Life was pulling her in a dozen different directions.

Not all the distractions were pleasant. Bonnie's father was sick. Charlie Blair, who had taught his little girl to dream of the Olympics, had lung cancer. Still, he continued to help speed skaters. On December 23, he timed skaters at a meet in Milwaukee. Two days later, on Christmas Day 1989, he died.

In a salute to her father's memory, Bonnie won all four races at the national championships two weeks later in Butte.

The season before the Olympics is always an important one for speed skaters. Everyone wants to race well and gain confidence for the Games. For Bonnie, however, the 1990-91 season was full of problems. She was sick with bronchitis most of the winter. And because of the Persian Gulf War, American athletes were afraid of attacks by terrorists in Europe. Bonnie raced in Europe, and then flew back to the United States or Canada to train until her next meet. Then she flew back to Europe to race. Between her illness and all the traveling, Bonnie was always tired. At the world sprint speed skating championships in Inzell, Germany, the best Bonnie could do was fifth place overall—her worst finish since 1985.

Bonnie's parents had always told her not to be upset about the outcome of a skating race. Even though she loved to win, she knew it wasn't the end of the world if she lost. Bonnie quickly forgot about her disappointing season. In the summer of 1991, she regained her form and her confidence. Former Olympic champion Peter Mueller became her coach. Bonnie trained harder than ever before. Some days she lifted weights, or ran, or took a long bicycle ride. Coach Mueller measured out a 400-meter oval on a parking lot at Milwaukee County Stadium so she could practice while wearing in-line skates.

Peter Mueller coached Bonnie before the 1992 Olympics.

When the competitive season began, Bonnie was once again the skater to beat. In dozens of 500- and 1,000-meter races leading up to the Olympics, Bonnie went undefeated. At the U.S. Olympic trials, Bonnie had nine races and won eight times. (She finished second in a 1,500-meter race because her skate blade broke.) Still, she wasn't satisfied. Bonnie was trying to get better in each race so that she would be at her very best for the Olympics.

"I've tried to go with only one peak this year," Bonnie said during the trials. "Hopefully, you haven't seen the best of Bonnie yet this year."

Once she arrived in Albertville, France, Bonnie didn't have much time to think about her Olympic strategy. Her first race, the 500 meters, was just two days after the opening ceremony.

Bonnie's chief rival was Ye Qiaobo of China. Ye had hoped to challenge Bonnie in 1988, but was sent home in disgrace after a pre-Olympic drug test showed that Ye used drugs that gave her an unfair advantage. Ye said the drugs were in a medicine her coach had given her. Another skater who would be a medal threat was Christa Rothenburger Luding, who had finished second to Bonnie in the Calgary Games. She had a new name (Luding) because she got married after the 1988 Olympics, and she was competing for a different team (Germany) because East and West Germany had been reunited as one country.

Fans by the thousands packed into the speed skating oval for the race. Among them were 44 relatives and friends of Bonnie's. They had come from 16 states to see the Olympics! For good luck, Bonnie ate a peanut butter-and-jelly sandwich before the race. Maybe the result would be as good as it had been in Calgary when she'd eaten PB&Js before competing.

As the first few pairs skated, Bonnie realized she would have a real test on her hands. Ye nearly bumped into the skater she was paired with when they switched lanes on the crossing straight. Still, Ye's final time of 40.51 seconds put her in first place. Then, Luding used an explosive start to finish in 40.57.

Finally, the fifth pair of the day—Bonnie's pair—was called to the line. Bonnie was assigned to the inside lane with Angela Hauck of Germany to her right.

"Go to the start," ordered the starter. "Ready," he barked. The skaters crouched low to the ice. Then he fired the gun and Bonnie was off. She ran down the ice a few steps, then began skating with powerful strokes. Bonnie reached the 100-meter split in 10.71 seconds—the fastest time of the day! And she got even faster from there. With each stride, Bonnie was closer to Olympic history. Would she become the first woman to win back-to-back gold medals in the 500 meters?

Bonnie crossed the finish line and the scoreboard clock froze at 40.33 seconds. Yes! Bonnie had beaten the times of Ye and Luding to repeat as Olympic champion. Bonnie pulled down the hood of her uniform and skated to the backstretch of the oval. Her boyfriend, David Cruikshank, and Coach Mueller slapped her hands. In the crowd, Bonnie's cheering section went wild. Someone accidentally knocked off the gold baseball cap Bonnie's mom was wearing. But who cared? Bonnie was Number 1!

Bonnie showed her emotional side at the news conference following her victory. She cried as she talked about her father.

"It was my dad's dream that I'd be in the Olympics before it was ever my dream," Bonnie told the reporters. "He'd always say, 'You're going to go win a gold medal.' I always thought he was crazy.

"I was glad he was with me in 1988 and he was there to see that," Bonnie continued, her voice cracking with emotion, "but this medal definitely goes to him."

Two days later, Bonnie skated in the 1,500 meters, her least favorite event. By the last lap of the 3¾-lap race, she was off the pace she would need to win a medal. Bonnie's coach signaled her to back off and conserve her strength for the 1,000 meters later in the week.

Bonnie was on top again in Albertville.

Maybe she could win a medal in the 1,000 if she didn't burn up all her energy in the 1,500. Bonnie wound up five seconds slower than the 1,500-meters winner and placed 21st.

After two Olympic Games, Bonnie had three gold medals.

Coach Mueller's strategy in the 1,500 proved to be right when Bonnie competed in the 1,000 meters. Bonnie, skating in the third pair of the day, attacked the race and had the fastest times for the first 200 and 600 meters, called split times, of the race. Her final time was 1 minute, 21.90 seconds, a record for the Albertville oval.

Bonnie knew she couldn't celebrate yet. Other good skaters still had a shot at the gold medal. In the stands, Eleanor Blair wrote down the times of the other competitors so she could compare them to Bonnie's.

Three pairs later, Ye and Germany's Monique Garbrecht took the ice. Their 600-meter split times were slower than Bonnie's, but not by much. Although her form faltered in the last lap, Ye's time was just two-hundredths of a second slower than Bonnie's. Bonnie had won again! If Ye and Bonnie had competed in the same pair, Bonnie would have won by the length of a skate blade—the same margin by which she had won her 500-meter gold medal in Calgary. "It's not very much, but it's enough to win," said Bonnie, "so I'll take it."

As the Albertville Olympics ended, people were wondering if Bonnie would retire from competition. Some thought that Bonnie should take advantage of a quirk in the Olympic schedule. The Winter and Summer Olympics had been held in the same year, every four years. In 1986, the International Olympic Committee had decided to have the Winter Olympics and Summer Olympics in different years. There would still be four years between Winter Games and four years between Summer Games, but there would be an Olympics every two years. The Olympic Committee decided to begin the new schedule with the Winter Olympics in 1994—just two years after Bonnie's gold-medal performance in 1992.

Soon Bonnie announced her decision. She would "go for the gold" one more time.

Bonnie had a new place to train when the Pettit National Ice Center opened in Milwaukee in 1992. The huge building holds three skating rinks.

Lillehammer and Beyond

Years of hard training, the support of her family, and even peanut butter-and-jelly sandwiches had been part of Bonnie's success stories in 1988 and 1992. As she prepared for the 1994 Olympics, Bonnie had something else in her favor—a new practice rink.

At the same time Bonnie was competing in Albertville and winning two gold medals, a new indoor skating rink was being built in Milwaukee. Now, no matter what the weather was like, Bonnie could do her workouts. "That wind can blow all it wants," she said.

Bonnie had a new coach too. Peter Mueller had coached Bonnie at the Olympics in Albertville in 1992. But Bonnie was not satisfied with her races after the Olympics. She thought a different coach could help her skate as fast as she had in 1988, when she set the world record in the 500 meters.

Above, Bonnie's team-mates on the 1984, 1988, and 1992 Olympic teams had included Dan Jansen (left) and Nick Thometz (center). At left, Nick Thometz became Bonnie's coach in 1993.

Bonnie chose Nick Thometz as her new coach. The first thing Coach Thometz did was change Bonnie's workout schedule for the summer. He knew Bonnie would work hard, so he made the practices shorter and more intense. She trained four days in a row, then rested one day. When Peter Mueller was her coach, Bonnie worked out six days before she got a day off.

Soon, it became clear that Bonnie was benefiting from Coach Thometz's plan. Even though she suffered a minor injury early in the 1993-94 season, she lost only one 500-meter race.

Bonnie won all four races to capture the overall gold medal at the 1994 world sprint speed skating championships in Canada. Three weeks later, the Olympic Games began in Lillehammer, Norway.

The speed skating races were in Hamar, a city about 20 miles from Lillehammer. Organizers built an enormous enclosed oval there, named the Hamar Olympic Hall. People called it the Viking Ship, however, because its roof looked like an upside-down boat.

The athletes were eager to race at the Viking Ship because the rink was fast. In the first week of Olympic competition, some of the skaters went so fast they had problems. Bonnie's teammate, Dan Jansen, slipped in the men's 500 meters and missed earning a medal. Gunda Niemann, a German skater who was expected to win a gold medal, fell in the women's 3,000 meters and didn't place among the top three.

Bonnie was able to put the other skaters' bad luck out of her mind. She didn't even attend most of the races. Instead, she concentrated on her first event, the 500 meters. "She's as confident as she's ever been," said Coach Thometz.

Just like in Calgary and Albertville, Bonnie had a big group of friends and family members at the Olympics. There were about 60 of them at the 500-meter race. They all wore sweatshirts that read "The Blair Bunch" and shiny gold baseball caps that read "Go Bonnie Gold." Bonnie's mom sat right in the middle of the front row.

Many of the skaters Bonnie competed against in Albertville had retired from racing. Younger women who considered Bonnie their hero now were trying to beat her. One of them was Franziska Schenk of Germany, who was 19 years old—10 years younger than Bonnie.

Schenk skated in the second pair of the day and recorded a time of 39.71 seconds. That wasn't close to Bonnie's world-record time, but it was the fastest time of the day until Bonnie skated.

Two pairs after Schenk, Bonnie went to the starting line. She kicked the ice to make a little hole in it, then put the toe of her left skate in the hole.

The Blair Bunch, Bonnie's relatives and friends, wore shiny gold caps as they cheered for Bonnie in Lillehammer.

Bonnie looked down the track and let out a big breath. She leaned forward and waited for the gun. Silence gripped the crowd.

Bonnie's first 100 meters gave her fans plenty of reason to yell. Her time was 10.60 seconds, the fastest she had skated all year. With every stroke, Bonnie increased her lead over the skater with whom she was paired, Germany's Monique Garbrecht.

Bonnie made it three in a row when she won the 500-meter gold in Norway.

As Bonnie closed in on the finish line, the Blair family watched the clock. They cheered wildly when they saw Bonnie's time—39.25 seconds, enough to pass Schenk and take the lead. Bonnie clapped and gave a thumbs-up to the crowd. But she didn't celebrate too much because other good skaters hadn't raced yet.

Pair by pair, skaters tried to knock Bonnie out of first place. Some of them had faster 100-meter times than Bonnie's, but they tired late in the race. When the results were final, the second-place skater was more than three-tenths of a second slower than Bonnie. The 500-meter gold medal was Bonnie's for the third time in a row.

Bonnie couldn't wait to share her victory with her fans. Still wearing her skates, she climbed up into the bleachers and began celebrating. Bonnie had a special hug for her brother Rob because it was his birthday.

Two days later, Bonnie skated in the 1,500 meters. That race is always one of the most interesting in the Olympics because it is too long to be a sprint and too short to be a distance event. For Bonnie to win a medal, she would have to sprint at the beginning of the race and try to maintain her form over the final lap.

Bonnie skated hard for as long as she could. Her legs were aching and her lungs were burning as she completed the race. Her time was excellent— 2 minutes, 3.44 seconds. She had skated the fastest 1,500 meters an American woman had ever skated. Would it be good enough for an Olympic medal?

Bonnie was in third place by three-hundredths of a second until Russia's Svetlana Fedokina skated the second-best time of the day. Fedokina's time bumped Bonnie into fourth place. After the race, Bonnie reminded her fans of the two Olympic gold medals she had won by only two-hundredths of a second. "It [winning the bronze medal] would have been nice, but the girls ahead of me skated great races," she said, as gracious in defeat as she had been in victory.

Now there was just one race left in Bonnie's Olympic career—the 1,000 meters. The first pair of the day featured Yoo Sun-Hee of Korea, the only skater to beat Bonnie in the 500 meters all season. Yoo was good at the 1,000, too. Her time of 1:21.40 gave the other women a target.

Bonnie was in the second pair with Ye Qiaobo, the Chinese skater who had finished second to her in Albertville by just two-hundredths of a second. After a quick start, Bonnie faltered briefly about halfway through the race. She slipped and had to put her left hand down on the ice to keep her balance. She recovered quickly, however, and finished in 1:18.74, the second-fastest 1,000-meters time of her career and 1.38 seconds ahead of Yoo's time.

Ye wasn't even close, and neither were any of the competitors who followed. Bonnie's margin of victory was the largest ever in a women's Olympic 1,000-meter race. Bonnie and Coach Thometz hugged and cried and laughed. Olympic history! Five gold medals!

At the medals ceremony, Bonnie blinked back tears. Smiling broadly, she sang along to "The Star-Spangled Banner" as the American flag flew overhead. With tears in their eyes, her mother and the rest of the Blair Bunch sang, too.

Bonnie's memorable day ended with a special lap on the Viking Ship ice. Thousands of fans cheered as Bonnie skated around the oval. She wore her brother Rob's "Go Bonnie Gold" cap, her newest gold medal, and gold laces in her skates. She was gold from head to toe.

Bonnie said she planned to keep competing after the Olympics and end her career at the 1995 World Sprint speed skating championships in Milwaukee. Then she would finish her physical education and business degree and begin coaching young skaters. The woman who skated circles around her competition plans to pass along that golden touch.

Bonnie Blair's Career Highlights

YEAR	MEET	EVENT	TIME/SCORE	FINISH
1984	Olympics	500 meters	42.53 seconds	8
1986	World Short-Track	overall	18 points	1
1986	World Sprints	overall	163.635 points	3
1987	World Sprints	overall	167.810 points	2
1988	World Sprints	overall	167.495 points	3
1988	Olympics	500 meters	39.10	1
1988	Olympics	1,000 meters	b–1:18.31	3
1988	Olympics	1,500 meters	b–2:03.89	4
1989	World Sprints	overall	a–159.435 points	1
1990	World Sprints	overall	165.395 points	2
1991	World Sprints	overall	164.015 points	5
1992	Olympics	500 meters	40.33	1
1992	Olympics	1,000 meters	1:21.90	1
1992	Olympics	1,500 meters	2:10.89	21
1992	World Sprints	overall	168.790 points	2
1993	World Sprints	overall	166.475 points	2
1994	World Sprints	overall	a–157.405 points	1
1994	Olympics	500 meters	39.25	1
1994	Olympics	1,000 meters	1:18.74	1
1994	Olympics	1,500 meters	b–2:03.44	4
1994	Olympic Oval Finale	500 meters	a–38.99	1

a–World and American record; b–American record
Note: In the World Sprint Speed Skating Championships, point totals are determined by times. The lower the score, the better

Major Awards and Honors

1992: Winner of the Sullivan Award, given annually by the Amateur Athletic Union to the nation's leading amateur athlete

U.S. Olympic Committee Sports Woman of the Year

ABC Sports Athlete of the Year

Clairol Personal Best Award

American Academy of Achievement Award

Oscar Statuett Award/International Speed Skater of the Year (first female recipient)

1988: Chicago Sports Hall of Fame Distinguished Achievement Award

Victor Award/Female Athlete of the Year

1987: Outstanding Women in America

1986: Women's Sports Foundation Up & Coming Award

ABOUT THE AUTHOR

In 1994, Cathy Breitenbucher began her third decade as a professional journalist. She spent 10 years as a sports writer for the Milwaukee Sentinel, where her assignments included the 1984 and 1988 Olympic Games. She became a freelance writer and editor in 1992. Cathy lives in the Milwaukee area with her husband and daughter.

ACKNOWLEDGMENTS

Photographs are reproduced with the permission of: pp. 1, 10, 27, 31, 40, 42, 44, 45, 47, © William Meyer; p. 2, Simon Bruty / Allsport Photography, Inc.; pp. 6, 58, Shaun Botterill / Allsport Photography, Inc.; pp. 9, 28, 35, 52, 54 (top), Photo Action USA / Cy White; p. 12, Rick Stewart / Allsport Photography, Inc.; pp. 16, 17, 18, 20, 39, Eleanor Blair; p. 23, © Tony Inzerillo; p. 33, Mike Powell / Allsport Photography, Inc.; p. 37, G. Mortimore / Allsport Photography, Inc.; p. 49, Bob Martin / Allsport Photography, Inc.; p. 50, SportsChrome East / West, Rob Tringali Jr.; pp. 54 (bottom), 57, SportsChrome East / West, Jeff Crow; p. 61, Chris Cole / Allsport Photography, Inc.; pp. 62, 64, © Cathy Breitenbucher.

Front cover photographs by Shaun Botterill / Allsport Photography, Inc., and Tim Defrisco / Allsport Photography, Inc. Back cover photograph by Rick Stewart / Allsport Photography, Inc.